Handy New York Genealogy Handbook

I0450655

By Gary L. Morris

©2015 Gary L. Morris

ISBN-13: 978-1506180120

ISBN-10: 1506180124

Table of Contents

Genealogical Research in New York State

Home to one of the first immigrant settlements in America, and one of the country's all time most popular ports of entry, it's quite possible that the "Empire State" could hold some answers to your ancestry. But with a population of nearly 20 million, and a history stretching back four hundred years, finding your ancestor there will require a consummate strategy. The racial, religious, and cultural demographics of New York State however, add to its richness of character, and make for fertile researching grounds for family historians.

We have sought high and low to find you the very best resources and the most accurate information available for doing genealogical research in New York State, both online and off. There are and abundance of genealogical records available for New York, and we'll show you:

1.   What they are
2.   Where to find them
3.   How to use them

Initially we're going to cover the early history and settlement of New York State. Knowing where its population came from, where they settled, and where they may have migrated to is valuable information to the genealogical researcher. That type of knowledge can direct you as to where you should look for a particular surname, even what period to search for it in.

A Brief Genealogical History of New York

It is believed the earliest inhabitants of New York State arrived in the area around 12,000 years ago. These peoples grew into what became the Algonquian and Iroquoian cultures, which included the Iroquois, Mohawk and Cherokee nations. The first Europeans to discover New York were the French, who arrived in 1524, but the first to lay claim to the land were the Dutch in 1609.

The Dutch initially made up the majority of New York's population, and this remained so until the 18th century. By that time colonists from England had settled, and the Pilgrims of New England slowly began to migrate into Long Island and Staten Island by way of Connecticut. Others expanded into the areas that are modern day Westchester and Albany.

Revolutions across the European continent in1848 saw many liberalist Germans arrive in New York during that year. The Germans immigrants were generally warmly received, and established shops, schools, newspapers, and some like Carl Schurz (US Senator and Secretary to the Interior) became political leaders. In the 1850's alone more than three quarters of a million Germans passed through New York via Ellis Island, and established communities such as Little Germany (now Alphabet City, Manhattan), and Yorkville on the Upper East Side.

The bulk of Irish immigrants began arriving during the 1850's, but they were present in smaller numbers before that time. Irish names have been found on some of the ancient registers of the Dutch Reformed Church, and the Earl of Limerick. Irish continued to immigrate to the New World throughout the Revolutionary War period, and following the War of 1812, a steady stream of them made their way to American shores. The greatest numbers came during the course of the Great Famine, and soon made up a quarter of the east coast population, many of them settling in Lower Manhattan

The Italians weren't as warmly welcomed as the Germans and Protestant Irish, and so clustered together in their own small communities as a matter of survival. Over 600,000 Italian immigrants arrived in New York between 1890 and 1900, most of them from southern Italy and Sicily.

Jewish immigrants arrived in the wake of the Germans and Irish in the late nineteenth century. Many came from the Russian Empire of that era, which would have included Lithuania, the Ukraine, Poland and other Russian satellite nations.

Important Genealogical Dates in New York History

1625 – New Amsterdam founded by the Dutch West India Company.

1674 – The Dutch cede New York permanently to England after the Third Anglo-Dutch War.

1702 – Yellow fever epidemic kills more than 500 people.

1783 – New Yorkers celebrate Evacuation Day, the day George Washington returned to the city and the last British forces left the United States.

1795 – Yellow fever epidemic kills 732

1798 – The "great epidemic", a major yellow fever epidemic, kills 2086 people

1805 – Yellow fever epidemic, during which as many as 50,000 people are said to have fled the city.

1832 – Cholera pandemic breaks out in New York City on June 26, peaks at 100 deaths per day during July, and finally abates in December. More than 3500 people die in the city, another 80,000 people, one third of the population, are said to have fled the city during the epidemic.

1863 – Approximately 50,000 people riot in protest of President Abraham Lincoln's announcement of a draft for troops to fight in the American Civil War. Over 100 are killed and many African Americans flee the city. The movie Gangs of New York takes place during the draft riots.

1918 – The "Great Influenza Pandemic" rages across the country and worldwide. On one particularly virulent October day, 851 people died in New York City alone.

September 11, 2001 – The two 110-story World Trade Center towers and several surrounding buildings are destroyed by two jetliners in part of a coordinated terrorist attack by radical Terrorists ("9/11"). In 2004, the count of the dead in New York City alone from the 9/11 attacks is set at over 2,600 people.

Famous Battles Fought in New York

New York played a crucial and decisive role in America's wars for independence. The Patriot victory at the **Battle of Saratoga** turned the tide of the entire war effort and was a major factor in attracting the assistance from the French which led to the triumphant victory of the Continental Army.

Battle of Saratoga: http://www.history.com/topics/american-revolution/battle-of-saratoga

Control of the Hudson River was vital to the war effort on both sides. The British held New York City and its port for most of the war; the Continental Army controlled most of the Hudson River, allowing them access to the entire Hudson Valley. The Hudson River provided a vital escape route for Washington's army after the **Battle of Brooklyn** and ensured that the Continental Army would live to fight again.

Battle of Brooklyn: http://www.history.com/this-day-in-history/the-battle-of-brooklyn

Nearly one third of all the battles fought during the American Revolution were fought in New York State. The **Siege of Fort Ticonderoga**, and the **Battle of Oriskany** are just a few of the major events that took place on New York soil. The **Battle of Long Island** was the largest of the American Revolution and the first fought after the Declaration of Independence.

Siege of Fort Ticonderoga: http://www.history.com/topics/american-revolution/capture-of-fort-ticonderoga

Battle of Oriskany: http://www.history.com/this-day-in-history/general-nicholas-herkimer-falls-at-the-battle-of-oriskany

Battle of Long Island: http://www.britishbattles.com/long-island.htm

Other important battles fought in New York state are: The **Battle of White Plains**, The **Battle of Fort Washington**, and The **Battle of Bennington**.

Battle of White Plains: http://www.landofthebrave.info/battle-of-white-plains.htm

Battle of Fort Washington:
http://www.theamericanrevolution.org/battledetail.aspx?battle=13

Battle of Bennington: http://www.britishbattles.com/battle-bennington.htm

Common New York State Genealogical Issues and Resources to Overcome Them

Boundary Changes: A major issue in researching ancestors in New York State are historical boundary changes. It is common to be searching for an ancestor's record in one county when in fact it is stored in a different one due to county boundaries being changed. The **Atlas of Historical County Boundaries** can help you to overcome that problem. It provides a chronological listing of every boundary change that has occurred in the history of New York State.

Atlas of Historical County Boundaries:
http://publications.newberry.org/ahcbp/documents/NY_Consolidated
_Chronology.htm#Consolidated_Chronology

Name Changes: Surname changes, variations, and misspellings can complicate genealogical research. It is important to check all spelling variations. Soundex, a program that indexes names by sound, is a useful first step, but you can't rely on it completely as some name variations result in different Soundex codes. The surnames could be different, but the first name may be different too. You can also find records filed under initials, middle names, and nicknames as well, so you will need to **get creative with surname variations** and spellings in order to cover all the possibilities. For help with surname variations read our instructional article on **How to Use Soundex**.

get creative with surname variations:
http://obituarieshelp.org/blog/?p=634

How to Use Soundex link to: http://obituarieshelp.org/blog/?p=505

New York Genealogical Organizations and Archives

As would be expected, New York State is home to a vast array of genealogical records. These historical documents are housed and maintained by a variety of organizations and institutions, ranging from the State Archives to private Genealogical Societies. The State is a genealogist's paradise, with a number of museums and universities also containing databases of precious genealogical and historical information. Following are links to their websites, their physical addresses, and a summary of the records you can find there.

Archives

New York State Archives - The State Archives of New York was born in 1971 though the general public had no access until 1978. It is headquartered in Albany at the Cultural Education Centre on the state capitol's Madison Avenue, and operated by the Education Department of New York. More than 200 million documents are stored at the State Archives, documenting the cities growth and populace form the 1600's to present day.

New York State Archives
New York State Education Department
Cultural Education Center
Albany, NY 12230

Research Assistance
Tel: (518) 474-8955
Email: archref@mail.nysed.gov

New York State Archives:
http://www.archives.nysed.gov/aindex.shtml

New York State Department of Health - The New York State Department of Health has a Vital Records section in which they file certificates for births and deaths occurring in the State of New York outside of New York City and marriage licenses that were issued in New York State also beyond New York City. They also maintain divorce records for the entire State dating from 1963. The local Municipality where the event occurred will also house birth and death records, while marriage records can be obtained from the municipality's Town or City Clerk where the licence was issued.

New York State Department of Health
Corning Tower
Empire State Plaza,
Albany, NY 12237

Email: vr@health.state.ny.us

New York State Department of Healtho:
http://www.health.ny.gov/vital_records/

New York State Municipal Archives - Records date from the early 1600's to present day and include vital records, census reports, city directories, business records, manuscripts, maps, sound recordings, and images. There are also records related to criminal justice administration that date from 1684 – 1966. Some of the oldest records here are legislative records which date back to the time of the first Dutch colonial government, while there are also mayoral records which have recorded the history of New York since 1849 that boast a wealth of in-depth information about the city.

Department of Records and Information Services
31 Chambers Street
New York, NY 10007

Email: Via online contact form

New York State Municipal Archives:
http://www.nyc.gov/html/records/html/archives/archives.shtml

Some important Historical Records Repositories in New York State that have archives with a searchable online catalogue are:

Franklin D. Roosevelt Presidential Library and Museum – manuscripts, historical documents, historical photographs, audio/visual collections, rare and historical books

511 Albany Post Road
Hyde Park NY, 12538
Tel: 845-486-7742
Email: archives.fdr@nara.gov

Franklin D. Roosevelt Presidential Library and Museum:
http://www.fdrlibrary.marist.edu/

Schomburg Center for Research in Black Culture - manuscripts and archival collections related to the performing arts, women, manuscripts and research files of historians and other scholars, Harlem, African American writers, records of civil rights organizations and individuals and organizations documenting radical political movements, religion, and eighteenth and nineteenth century Haitian history. Rare book collection includes narratives and studies in slavery and anti-slavery movements in the United States

515 Malcolm X Boulevard
New York NY, 10037
Tel: 212-491-2224

Schomburg Center for Research in Black Culture:
http://www.nypl.org/locations/schomburg

Columbia University Special Collections and Archives – books, periodicals, historical records.

435 West 116th St.
New York NY, 10027
Tel: 212-854-5244
Fax: 212-854-3295

Columbia University Special Collections and Archives link to: http://library.columbia.edu/locations/eastasian/special_collections.html

Genealogical and historical societies have access to extensive catalogues of genealogical data. They are also able to offer expert guidance for genealogical researchers. Many members are professional genealogists who are most willing to share their expertise in finding ancestors.

New York State Genealogical and Historical Societies

Central New York Genealogical Society – county records, surname database, research support.

Box 104 Colvin Station
Syracuse, NY 13205

Central New York Genealogical Society:
http://www.rootsweb.ancestry.com/~nycnygs/

New York Genealogical & Biographical Society – county guides, census reports, marriage and death record abstracts, religious records, cemetery transcriptions, Harlem cemetery internments.

122 East 58th Street
New York, NY 10022
Tel: (212) 755-8532

New York Genealogical & Biographical Society:
http://www.newyorkfamilyhistory.org/

New York Historical Society – historical records, newspaper collection, maps, atlases, manuscripts, business records, manuscripts relating to slavery and African American history, Revolutionary War era, Civil War materials, and other historical resources.

170 Central Park West
New York, NY 10024
Tel: (212) 873-3400

New York Historical Society: http://www.nyhistory.org/

New York State Family History Centers

There are over 50 Family History Centers run by the Latter Day
Saints (LDS) in New York, and they are a stalwart of genealogical
research. The LDS have accumulated billions of genealogical
records from as far back as the early 17th century; in fact it is the
largest collection of vital data in the world. At the online directory
for **LDS Family History Centers** you will find Addresses and
contact information for LDS Family History Centers in New York
State

LDS Family History Centers:
http://www.familysearch.org/eng/library/FHC/frameset_fhc.asp

Additional New York State Genealogical Resources

New York State Mailing Lists

Mailing lists are internet based facilities that use email to distribute a single message to all who subscribe to it. When information on a particular surname, new records, or any other important genealogy information related to the mailing list topic becomes available, the subscribers are alerted to it. Joining a mailing list is an excellent way to stay up to date on New York State genealogy topics. Rootsweb have an extensive listing of **New York State Mailing Lists** on a variety of topics.

New York State Mailing Lists:
http://bigfile.rootsweb.ancestry.com/cgi-bin/listsearch

New York State Message Boards

A message board is another internet based facility where people can post questions about a specific genealogy topic and have it answered by other genealogists. If you have questions about a surname, record type, or research topic, you can post your question and other researchers and genealogists will help you with the answer. The **Message Boards at Rootsweb** are completely free to use.

Message Boards at Rootsweb:
http://boards.rootsweb.com/localities.northam.usa.states/mb.ashx

Newspapers and Periodicals

New York Historical Newspapers - Digitized New York newspapers from 1803-2013

New York Historical Newspapers:
http://nyshistoricnewspapers.org/

New York State Library - All New Yoek newspapers known to exist have been catalkogued and microfilmed.

Cultural Education Center
222 Madison Avenue
Albany, NY 12230
Tel: 1 518-474-5355

New York State Library (Alphabetical Listing):http://www.nysl.nysed.gov/nysnp/title4.htm

Rochester Public Library - The Rochester Newspaper Index is a project of the Rochester Public Library; database consists of references to articles that appeared in the Rochester newspapers during the period 1818-1897. Indexed in two time periods: 1818 – 1850 and 1851 – 1897.

Rochester Newspaper Index:
http://www3.libraryweb.org/lh.aspx?id=963&ekmensel=c57dfa7b_1 2_38_963_9

New York Heritage Digital Collection - St. Lawrence County newspapers from mid 19th century.

New York Heritage Digital Collection:
http://www.nyheritage.org/newspapers/county/stlawrence

Library of Congress US Newspaper Directory - Historical newspapers dating from 1690 for every US state

Library of Congress US Newspaper Directory: http://chroniclingamerica.loc.gov/search/titles/

American Periodicals (1740-1940) - searchable full-text and page images from over 1,800 popular magazines, journals and newspapers which began publication between 1740 and 1900 with coverage through 1940. Also contains titles archived at the **Center for Research Libraries** (CRL), including labor, trade, literary, scientific, and photographic periodicals, as well as other historically-significant titles.

American Periodicals: http://www.nypl.org/collections/articles-databases/american-periodical-series-online

Center for Research Libraries: http://www.crl.edu/

New York University Libraries - Historical journals from 1639

New York University Libraries: http://guides.nyu.edu/content.php?pid=34183&sid=1301966

Historical New York State Maps and Gazetteers

Maps help us to locate landmarks, towns, cities, parishes, states, provinces, waterways and roads and streets. They also help us to determine when and where boundary changes might have taken place, and give us a visualization of the area we're researching in. For locating place names, a gazetteer is the best possible resource for any genealogist. Below are links to the maps and gazetteers for research in New York State.

Peabody GNIS Service – New York State: http://peabody.research.yale.edu/cgi-bin/Query.GNIS?ST=New%20York&SU=1

1985 U.S. Atlas: http://www.livgenmi.com/1895/NY/

Color Landform Atlas: http://fermi.jhuapl.edu/states/ny_0.html

New York State Hometown Locator: http://newyork.hometownlocator.com/

New York State City and County Directories

Although local historical and genealogical societies may prove the best resources for these valuable genealogical materials, you can also find them at the following institutions.

New York State Library - an excellent source for New York State city and county directories and other county and state-related information.

New York State Library;
http://www.nysl.nysed.gov/ils/topics/local.htm

New York City, New York Online Historical Directories – links to county and city directories from the early 17th century to the 1960's.

New York City, New York Online Historical Directories:
https://sites.google.com/site/onlinedirectorysite/Home/usa/ny/ne
wyorkcity

Fold3 - online Directories for Buffalo, Brooklyn, New York City, and Rochester

Fold3: http://www.fold3.com/category_14/

New York State Genealogical Records

Birth, Death and Marriage Records

In New York State birth, death, marriage, and divorce records are issued by the **Department of Health** for births that occur in the state outside of New York City. As Civil Registration outside of New York City began only in 1881, there is no such documentation prior to that year.

Department of Health: http://www.health.ny.gov/vital_records/

Birth certificates for persons born in **New York City** are held by two different organizations, depending on their date of birth. If the birth occurred before 1910, those documents are held by the **New York City Municipal Archives**. Those born after that date are held by the New York City Department of Health and Mental Hygiene. Let's first explain the process with those held by the Municipal Archives.

New York City Municipal Archives:
http://www.nyc.gov/html/records/html/archives/archives.shtml

The **New York City Marriage Bureau** retains marriage licences for the five boroughs of New York City from 1930 to present.

New York City Marriage Bureau:
http://www.cityclerk.nyc.gov/html/marriage/marriage_bureau.shtml

For earlier records you must contact the clerks Office of the relevant borough as follows:

Brooklyn marriage certificates 1866 – 1937 and 1908 to present at *City Clerks Office* in Brooklyn, marriages 1847 – 1865 can also be obtained from the *Kings County Clerks Office* in Brooklyn.

Bronx marriage indexes 1898 – 1937 (film 1983782 ff.) and 1908 to present at the *City Clerk's Office* in the Bronx.

Staten Island 1908 to present at the *City Clerks Office* in Staten Island.

Queens marriage records 1881 – 1937 and 1908 to present at the *City Clerks Office in Kew Gardens*, and some from 1908 – 1919 at the *Queens County Clerks Office in Jamaica, Queens*.

Manhattan marriage records and index (film 1522995 ff.) 1866 – 1937 and 1908 to present at the *Municipal Archives in New York City*.

Additional sources for **Death Records** are:

Italian Genealogical Group –a free database of death indexes for the five boroughs of New York City from 1862 – 1948.

Italian Genealogical Group: http://www.italiangen.org/records-search/deaths.php

Guilderland Public Library Digital Collection – obituary and death notices from the Altamont Enterprise and Knowersville Enterprise newspapers from 1884 – 2008.

Guilderland Public Library Digital Collection: http://www.guilpl.org/digitalmedia/

New York Deaths and Burials, 1795-1952– index to burial and death records for New York State.

New York Deaths and Burials, 1795-1952: https://familysearch.org/learn/wiki/en/New_York_Deaths_and_Burials_(FamilySearch_Historical_Records)

Census Reports

Federal Census Records for New York State have been taken every ten years commencing in 1790. The earliest reports contain the least information, mostly names of householders, number of occupants, and number of slaves owned, though subsequent reports became more comprehensive.

Census reports are available to the general public from the years 1790 – 1939, although those from 1890 were destroyed in a warehouse fire in 1921, and only a fragment survived from Westchester and Suffolk Counties. A useful substitute for the 1890 census is the Veterans and Widows schedule for that year.

All New York State Census reports taken prior to 1915 are held by the individual counties, and can be located by contacting the county Clerk for the area you're interested in. Most of the indexes can be searched online at **FamilySearch.org**, while the **New York State Library** retains microfilm copies of those for individual counties, as well as Federal Reports up till 1930. Census reports since 1930 are still under the custody of the US Bureau of the Census, and information contained in those reports is only available to the individual it concerns.

FamilySearch.org:
http://familysearch.org/learn/wiki/en/New_York_Census#Online_Ne w_York_indexes_and_images

New York State Library:
http://www.nysl.nysed.gov/genealogy/nyscens.htm

New York State Church Records

New York is the home of nearly every religion in existence, and so to simplify the process of records research, we will address the research of records of the various denominations separately. Many religions have central repositories where their records can be found, and generally it is good practice to write the relative body a letter stating your interest in the particular record. Various religions and potential resources for them are as follows:

Roman Catholic - An exception to the rule, the majority of Catholic records are not held in central repositories. In order to find your ancestors records you need to determine the town where your relatives lived and the parish church they were members of. If you discover the parish is no longer in existence, the may be kept by the diocese or a bordering parish – the diocese chancellor can inform you as to where the records are currently held.
Contact information for each diocese can be found at **NYSCatholic.org**.: http://www.nyscatholic.org/

Baptist – Baptist Records can be found at the **American Baptist Historical Society** in Atlanta, Georgia. Appointments must be made for research purposes.

American Baptist Historical Society: http://abhsarchives.org/

Episcopal – Episcopalian records are held by the **Episcopal Diocese of New York**. There are also dioceses of Central New York, Albany, Rochester, Long Island, and Western New York. The Family History Library houses many Episcopal records for Western New York and many of these records are indexed in the **International Genealogical Index**.

Episcopal Diocese of New York: http://www.dioceseny.org/

International Genealogical Index:
https://familysearch.org/learn/wiki/en/International_Genealogical_In dex

Jewish – Most local congregation maintain their own files, so you again need to know where your ancestor would have attended synagogue, though **The American Jewish Historical Society** holds a significant number of archival collections useful to genealogical researchers.

The American Jewish Historical Society: http://www.ajhs.org/

Dutch Reformed – The **Archives of the Reformed Church in America** is the source for these records, and is located at the Gardner A. Sage Library of New Brunswick Theological Seminary.

Archives of the Reformed Church in America: https://www.rca.org/page.aspx?pid=230

Lutheran – **National Lutheran Council Library** at Gustavus Adolphus College

National Lutheran Council Library: https://gustavus.edu/library/archives/LCA/guides/LCA0023.php

Methodist – The **United Methodist Archives Center** houses Baptism and Membership records as well as well as Biographies and an online archive.

United Methodist Archives Center: http://www.gcah.org/site/pp.aspx?c=ghKJI0PHIoE&b=3590193

Moravian – The **Moravian Church Archives** maintains their archives in Bethlehem, Pennsylvania which contains records of baptisms of infants, adults who joined the church as adults, as well as marriages, and funerals.

Moravian Church Archives: http://www.moravianchurcharchives.org/

Presbyterian - Headquartered in Philadelphia, Pennsylvania, the **Presbyterian Historical Society** maintains a records management program serving the church's local congregations, national agencies, mid councils, as well as researchers, scholars and the genealogical community.

If your religion is not listed here, the **New York Genealogical and Biographical Society** possesses a huge database of searchable religious records from various denominations.

Presbyterian Historical Society: http://www.history.pcusa.org/

New York Genealogical & Biographical Society: http://www.newyorkfamilyhistory.org/

New York Military Records

New Yorkers have taken part in various military campaigns since the colonial era, and there are a number of places where their records can be found. Many New York State military records can be found in the **State Archives**. These include:

- Colonial Muster Rolls
- Revolutionary War Records
- War of 1812 Payroll and Claims Records
- Civil War Muster Roll Abstracts
- New York Regiment Registers
- Union Volunteer Records
- Spanish – American War Records
- World War 1 service Records and Roll of Honor abstracts
- New York State Militia Registers 1800 – 1909
- National Guard Muster Rolls 1878 – 1954 and National Guard Commissioned Officers 1800 – 1909

State Archives:
http://www.archives.nysed.gov/a/research/res_topics_military.shtml

New York State Military Museum and Veteran's Research Center - military museum and research center dedicated to collecting and preserving the history of New York's veterans and military units. Retains a vast library of military and state history, unit histories, photographs, diaries, newspaper clippings, individual service records and more. There is also an online collection that you can search for free which includes a vast register of officers who completed their service before 1858, and a listing of Congressional Medal of Honor Recipients from New York State.

New York State Military Museum and Veteran's Research Center: http://dmna.ny.gov/historic/mil-hist.htm

New York Military Records at the USGenWeb Archives Project - collection of online military records specifically regarding New York State Regiments and Soldiers that you can search for free. Collection consists of Revolutionary War Service Records, Black Soldiers Records, Pensions Records, Civil War Regimental Records, Civil War Letters and Diaries, Vietnam Casualty Records.

New York Military Records at the USGenWeb Archives Project: http://www.usgwarchives.net/ny/state/military/militarytoc.htm

New York State Cemetery Records

There is no shortage of New York State cemetery records, as an incredible amount have been transcribed and published.

Internment.net - maintains cemetery transcription compiled by their staff who constantly visit cemeteries and transcribe their records, as well as those of volunteer transcribers who generously donate their time and work. You can search cemetery records for nearly every county in the State and the search is completely free of charge.

Internment.net: http://www.interment.net/us/index.htm

New Horizons Genealogy - site specializing in cemetery records dated before 1940. Their records are transcribed from old cemeteries, grave yards, burial grounds, and abandoned burial plots. They also have a decent selection of Revolutionary War burial records of soldiers whose graves have been officially noted, located, or marked by the DAR (Daughters of the American Revolution).

New Horizons Genealogy:
http://www.newhorizonsgenealogicalservices.com/cemetery-records-new-york.htm

New York Tombstone Inscription Project – database of records from the 18th and 19th centuries; includes major cemeteries, as well as smaller family plots with only one headstone remaining.
.
New York Tombstone Inscription Project:
http://www.usgwtombstones.org/newyork/newyork.html

Northern New York Tombstone Transcription Project – Tombstone inscriptions from Clinton County, NY.

Northern New York Tombstone Transcription Project:
http://freepages.genealogy.rootsweb.ancestry.com/~frgen/clinton/clintonindex.htm

A useful resource for cemetery records for **New York City** are the Ledger volumes that records the burials of those interred in the City Cemetery (Potters Field) on Hart Island situated at the western extreme of Long Island Sound. These ledgers are held in the archives of the **New York City Department of Records** and contain the names, dates of death, date the burial took place, where the death occurred, the cause of death, and the grave number. They are not indexed, and the burials of infants and pre-mature babies are listed separately. Burials recorded are for the years 1881 – 1950's.

New York City Department of Records:
http://www.nyc.gov/html/records/html/archives/collections_cemeteri
es.shtml

New York State Obituaries

Obituaries can reveal a wealth about our ancestor and other relatives. You can search our **New York State Newspaper Obituaries Listings** from hundreds of New York State newspapers online for free.

New York State Newspaper Obituaries Listings:
http://obituarieshelp.org/new_york_newspaper_obituaries.html

New York State Wills and Probate Records

Wills and Probate records dating back to the late 16th century can be found in New York due to its long and industrious history. Before the 1680's though, wills were probated by aldermen and notary publics, and unfortunately there was no law demanding they be recorded as public documents

From the period 1656–1668, the inheritances of minors were overseen by appointed orphan masters. The surviving records from this period can be found at the **New York City Municipal Archives**, while the remainder are held in the Netherlands at the **Amsterdam Municipal Archives**. A few of these records, dating from the 1650's to 1852, mention people who emigrated to the New York and New Jersey area (formerly New Netherland), and include; copies of wills, burial records, settlements, and divisions of estates.

New York City Municipal Archives:
http://www.nyc.gov/html/records/html/archives/collections.shtml

Amsterdam Municipal Archives:
http://stadsarchief.amsterdam.nl/english/

The 1960's saw the records of the New York Surrogate's Court sent to Queen's College for microfilming, before being permanently housed in the **State Archives**. They are listed as Records of the New York Court of Probates and its Colonial Predecessors, 1664–1823, and the collection includes wills, accounts and administrations dating from1664 – 1823. Additional records from the Chancery Court are to be found at the New York County Courthouse under the auspices of the City Clerk.

State Archives:
http://www.archives.nysed.gov/a/research/res_tools_nysa_path_probate.shtml

The **New York State Library** has New York (State) Courts of Probate probated wills, 1665-1815

New York State Library: http://nysl.nysed.gov/uhtbin/035-archives/(N-Ar)J0038

New York State Immigration and Naturalization Records

New York City was the gateway for those immigrating to the New World. There are some existing colonial records held by the **State Archives – *Customs House Records*** dating from around 1730; however they do not include the names of passengers.

State Archives – *Customs House Records*:
http://www.nypl.org/archives/1711

The greatest source for immigration records are without a doubt the **Ellis Island Passenger Lists.**

Ellis Island Passenger Lists: http://www.ellisisland.org/

The **New York City Passenger Lists at the New York Public Library** – contains records from 1820–1957 that contain the names, ages, and countries of origin. After 1897 they usually give the last residence and final destination in the United States.

New York City Passenger Lists at the New York Public Library: http://www.nypl.org/collections/articles-databases/new-york-passenger-lists-1820-1957

<u>Native American Records</u>

U.S. National Archives Indian Census Rolls- Census rolls that were usually submitted each year by agents or superintendents in charge of Indian reservations, to the Commissioner of Indian Affairs dating from 1885-1940.

U.S. National Archives Indian Census Rolls: http://www.archives.gov/research/native-americans/

Access Genealogy – New York Native American census records, tribal histories, and much more

Access Genealogy: http://www.accessgenealogy.com/native/new-york-indian-tribes.htm

Records of the Bureau of Indian Affairs (BIA)

Records of the Bureau of Indian Affairs (BIA) link to: http://www.archives.gov/research/guide-fed-records/groups/075.html

Buffalo and Erie Count Library – Wide variety of resources for Native Americans in New York State

Buffalo and Erie Count Library: http://www.buffalolib.org/sites/default/files/pdf/genealogy/subject-guides/NativeGenealogy2014.pdf

American Indians Records Repository - records dating from the 1700s including trust, education and other historic Indian Affairs records

American Indian Records Repository
Meritex Enterprises
17501 West 98th Street
Lenexa, KS 66219
Phone: 913-888-0601

American Indians Records Repository link to:
http://www.doi.gov/ost/records_mgmt/american-indian-records-repository.cfm

Missing Matriarchs – Resources for Researching Female New York State Ancestors

Looking for female ancestors requires an adjustment of how we view traditional records sources. A woman's identity was often under that of her husband, and often individual records for them can be difficult to locate. The following resources are effective in locating female ancestors in New York State where traditional records may not reveal them.

<u>Marriage and Divorce Records</u>

The State Department of Health in Concord has the following indexes of marriages and divorces from county to state level on microfilm that can be very useful for finding female ancestors.

- New York Marriage Register, 1829-1887, (film 1671684 ff.) – Municipal Archives
- Brooklyn Marriage Certificates, 1866-1937, (film 1653852 ff.) – King's County Clerk's Office, Brooklyn
- Manhattan Marriage Records and index, 1866-1937 (film 1522995 ff.) – Municipal Archives
- Queens Marriage Records, 1881-1937, (film 1908328) – Queens County Clerk's Office
- Bronx Marriage Index, 1898-1937, (film 1983782 ff.) – City Clerk's Office, Bronx
- Albany (city) Marriages, 1847, 1870-1917, and Albany County, 1908-1936, City clerk's Office, Albany
- Buffalo County Marriages, 1811-1935, - Erie County Clerk's office, Buffalo
- Yonker Marriages, 1870-present, Health Center Building, Yonkers

Bibliographies

1. *In the Eyes of the Law; Women, Marriage and Property in 19th Century New York,* Norma Basch (Cornell University press, 1982).
2. *Women and Property in Colonial New York: The Transition From Dutch to English Law, 1643-1727,* Linda Briggs Biemer, (University of Michigan Press, 1983)
3. *Immigrant Women in the Land of Dollars; Life and Culture on the Lower East Side, 1890-1925,* Elizabeth Ewen, (New York Monthly Review Press, 1985)
4. *New Immigrant Women at Work; Italians and Jews in New York City, 1880-1905,* T and BB Caroli Kessner, (Journal of Ethnic Studies)
5. *Immigrant Life in New York City,* Ernst, Roberts, (Columbia University Press, 1949)

Selected Resources for New York State Women's History

Adirondack Women in History
5 Middle Road
PO Box 565
Willsboro, NY 12996

James Wheelock Clark library
Russell Sage College
45 Ferry St.
Troy, NY 12180

National Women's Hall of Fame
PO Box 335
Seneca Falls, NY 13148-0335

Common New York State Surnames

Adams, Alderman, Aldrich, Alexander, Allen, Andrews, Armstrong, Babcock, Baker, Barber, Barnes, Benjamin, Bennett, Bingham, Bishop, Bosworth, Brewer, Brooks, Brown, Burdick, Butterfield, Campbell, Casey, Chandler, Chapman, Church, Clark, Coates, Cole, Cook, Coon, Cottrell, Corbin, Crowley, Davis, Dean, DeVeaux, Dodge, Driscoll, Dunham, Earley, Elliot, Ely, Evans, Fairbanks, Farwell, Finch, Flanagan, Foster, Forbes, Fuller, Gee, German, Gilbert, Gleason, Gordon, Graves, Grey, Green, Gross, Hall, Hammond, Hardy, Harrington, Harris, Haskins, Hill, Hitchcock, Hooker, Horton, Hungerford, Hunt, Jackson, Jennings, Johnson, Jones, Kellogg, King, Kingsbury, Knight, Lee, Leonard, Lewis, Lowell, Madison, Marsh, Maxson, McCarthy, McDonald, Merrick, Miller, Mills, Moore, Murphy, Nicholls, Norton, O'Brien, Oliver, Osborn, Parker, Peck, Perrin, Perry, Peterson, Potter, Randolph, Reynolds, Rice, Rich, Robbins, Robinson, Rogers, Sanford, Scott, Sherman, Sherwood, Slocum, Smith, Spencer, Stevens, Stuck, Swift, Taylor, Thomas, Ward, White, Wilcox, Williams, Wilson, Young

About the Author

Gary L. Morris worked from 2009 to 2014 as a professional researcher for a major player in the genealogy field. After tracing his family lineage back to 1683, he has decided to publish these helpful guides to share the valuable information he has discovered during his career to help others trace their family lineages. An avid genealogist himself, he hopes you will find this guide factual, thorough, helpful, and most of all, effective in helping you to find your family members.